Fact Finders®

A Primary Source History of
THE GOLD RUSH

by John Micklos, Jr.

Consultant: Richard Bell
Associate Professor of History
University of Maryland,
College Park

CAPSTONE PRESS
a capstone imprint

Fact Finders Books are published by Capstone Press,
1710 Roe Crest Drive, North Mankato, Minnesota 56003
www.mycapstone.com

Library of Congress Cataloging-in-Publication Data
Cataloging-in-Publication Data is on file with the Library of Congress..
ISBN 978-1-4914-8486-9 (library binding)
ISBN 978-1-4914-8490-6 (paperback)
ISBN 978-1-4914-8494-4 (eBook PDF)

Editorial Credits
Brenda Haugen, editor; Sarah Bennett, designer; Wanda Winch, media researcher;
Katy LaVigne, production specialist

Photo Credits
Corbis: Bettmann, cover (bottom); Courtesy of Pamela Dixon, 20; Getty Images: Archive Photos,
21, Mark Kauffman, 4, Transcendental Graphics, 13; Granger, NYC, 7; Library of Congress: Prints
and Photographs Division, 1 (bottom), 5, 17, 19; Newscom: Picture History, 25; North Wind Picture
Archives, 9, 12, 27; Science Source, 15; Shutterstock: dade72, 29, Philip Bird LRPS CPAGB, 6; The Art
Archives at Art Resource, N.Y., 23; Yale Collection of American Literature, Beinecke Rare Book and
Manuscript Library, cover (top), 1 (top), 11

Printed in the United States   5426

TABLE OF CONTENTS

A NOTE ABOUT PRIMARY SOURCES

Primary sources are newspaper articles, photographs, speeches, or other documents that were created during an event. They are great ways to see how people spoke and felt during that time. You'll find primary sources from the time of the Gold Rush throughout this book. Within the text, primary source quotations are colored *brown* and set in italic type.

A GLEAM IN THE RIVER

The California Gold Rush started by accident. James Marshall was building a **mill** beside the American River in northern California in early 1848. On January 24, as Marshall gazed down into the water of the **millrace**, he saw something gleaming. *"My eye was caught by something shining in the bottom of the ditch,"* he later recalled. *"I reached my hand down and picked it up."* That gleaming something was a piece of gold. Soon Marshall spotted more gold. He showed it to some of his workers. They did not believe the gold was real.

△ the original gold nugget James Marshall found

Marshall took the gold samples to John Sutter, who owned the mill property. Sutter tested them using simple tests from an encyclopedia. *"I declared this to be gold of the finest quality, of at least 23 carats,"* Sutter later wrote. The two men asked the workers at the mill site to keep the discovery a secret. Within weeks, however, word leaked out. Soon it spread to San Francisco, California. This small city of about 1,000 people was more than 100 miles (161 kilometers) away.

mill—a building with machines for turning wood, grain, or other materials into products
millrace—a channel that carries water to run a mill

△ James Marshall at Sutter's Mill, next to the American River in northern California

People in the 19th century talked about "seeing the elephant" when describing an event of great excitement. In the 1840s few people in the United States had ever seen an elephant. There were not yet any zoos in the nation. Few people had a chance to attend a circus. The phrase became linked with the excitement of traveling to California in search of gold.

California was sparsely settled in the 1840s. Of the 170,000 people living in California, nearly all were American Indians. Marshall's discovery changed the course of history for California. In fact, it affected the entire United States.

Spain had claimed the land, which it called Alta California, ever since its sailors first explored it in the 1500s. For a long time the region remained largely unsettled. Father Junipero Serra founded the first of 21 Spanish **missions** in California in 1769. Population growth was slow. Mexico was the nearest source of settlers. At the time, Spain ruled Mexico. But few Mexicans wanted to move to Alta California. American Indian tribes roamed most of the land.

"We have seen Indians in immense numbers," Serra wrote. He added that the American Indians made *"a good subsistence on various seeds, and by fishing."* Soon their way of life would change forever.

△ A statue honoring Junipero Serra stands in Santa Barbara, California.

mission—a church or other place where missionaries live and work
subsistence—a living, at a basic level

Mexico gained independence from Spain in 1822. At the same time, Spain gave control of Alta California to Mexico. The land became a Mexican territory. More Mexican settlers began arriving.

Over time a few U.S. citizens began trickling in as well. Some came from the East Coast by ship, sailing around the tip of South America. Several opened businesses in small towns along the California coast. Others became ranchers. Trappers came from the Midwest looking for beaver furs.

By the 1840s tensions between the Mexicans and Americans living in Alta California had grown. Both groups wanted control of the territory. Some of the Americans sought independence from Mexico in 1846. The rebels flew a flag with an image of a grizzly bear. Their movement became known as the Bear Flag Revolt.

▽   one of the original flags of the Bear Flag Revolt

As that small conflict was unfolding, the U.S. declared a broader war on Mexico. The war began over ownership of Texas, but U.S. President James Polk also hoped to gain control of California. He had tried to buy the land from Mexico, but Mexico refused to sell it. By July 1846 the American flag replaced the bear flag. Pioneer John Bidwell noted that the bear flag *"had no importance to begin with, none whatever when the Stars and Stripes went up."*

Although the U.S. had gained control of California, the territory still legally belonged to Mexico. But the outcome of the Mexican-American War would soon change that. U.S. troops captured the Mexican capital of Mexico City in 1847. Soon the fighting was over. The two nations began working on a peace treaty.

Meanwhile, California businessmen such as Sutter built stores and mills to meet the needs of settlers. The discovery of gold in 1848 sped up the region's growth. **Migration** and settlement that would normally take decades instead took place within just a few years.

Shortly after gold was discovered, the peace treaty ending the war between the U.S. and Mexico was signed. In the treaty Mexico gave vast territories to the U.S. for $15 million. These lands included present-day California. At the time neither the Mexican nor U.S. governments knew just how valuable this land would prove to be.

migration—movement of people

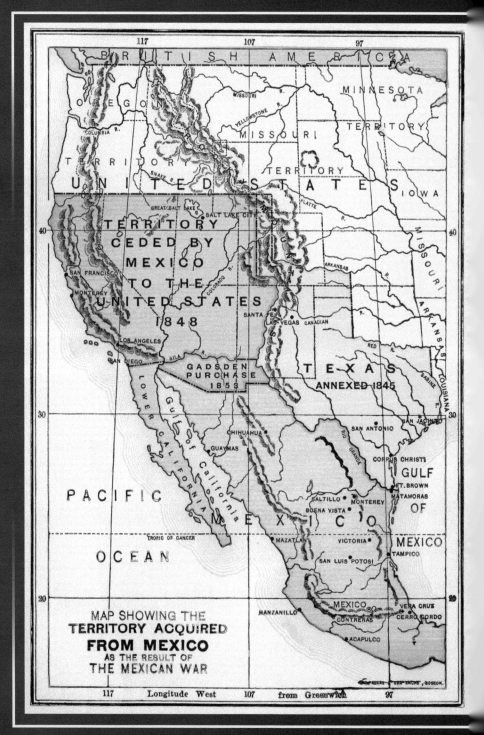

GOLD FEVER

News about the discovery of gold spread slowly at first. There were no telephones or email or even regular mail service. But businessman Sam Brannan wanted to spread news of the discovery. He owned a small store not far from the goldfields. He thought that if more people knew about the gold, his store would get more business.

Brannan bought pickaxes, shovels, pans, and other items miners would need. In May 1848 he traveled to San Francisco. Brannan went through the streets carrying a bottle filled with gold dust. *"Gold! Gold! Gold from the American River!"* he shouted. Within a few days most of San Francisco's population had left to search for gold. Brannan made a fortune selling mining supplies.

But Brannan wanted even more attention, and he used a newspaper he owned to get it. He printed a special issue that included an announcement of the gold discovery. *"From all accounts the mine is immensely rich,"* the article stated, *"and already, we learn, the gold from it is collected at random and without any trouble."* Brannan sent 2,000 copies of the special issue east by mule. He hoped to bring thousands of other miners to his store. The newspapers reached Missouri in July. From there, the news continued to slowly spread east.

A newspaper shared the story that gold was found in California.

The first gold seekers from outside California arrived in the spring and summer of 1848. They came from Oregon, Hawaii, and Mexico. Soon others seeking their fortunes came from Europe, China, Australia, and South America. News had reached them on boats traveling across the oceans.

By fall 1848 news of the gold discovery reached the eastern United States. Some people learned about it from Brannan's newspaper. Others heard reports from some of the early miners who had struck gold. Newspapers ran huge articles about the gold rush. The *Baltimore Sun* said: *"Rich Gold Fields Have Been Discovered in California!"* The *New York Herald* ran a story that said, *"The real **El Dorado** has at length been discovered."*

At first people found these stories hard to believe. But in December 1848, President James Polk said that the discoveries were likely real. *"Recent discoveries render it probable that these mines are more extensive and valuable than was anticipated,"* he said.

Many people took the dangerous overland journey west to California. Most expeditions left from towns along the Missouri River. The travelers crossed prairies, mountains, and deserts. Some faced attacks from **hostile** American Indian tribes. The tribes were angry about the number of people **trespassing** on their lands. About 9 out of 10 of the people heading to California in search of gold were men. A few brave women also traveled with their husbands. *"I thought where he could go I could, and where I went I could take my two little toddling babies,"* wrote Luzena Wilson.

△ Wagons and stagecoaches crossed the Sier Nevadas into California during the Gold Ru

hostile—unfriendly or angry
trespass—to go on another's property without permission

CRITICAL THINKING

Why do you think so few women and children traveled to California as part of the Gold Rush?

Tens of thousands of gold seekers journeyed to California in 1849. Many called themselves '49ers. Some sailed from New York and other East Coast cities by going around the tip of South America. That trip took several months. Others saved time by crossing Panama on foot. In Panama miners faced dense jungles, bugs, and disease. *"We were here attacked by one of the most ravenous swarms of musquitos it was ever my lot to encounter,"* said John M. Letts.

Gold seekers came from many parts of the world, but they all had one thing in common. They hoped to make a fortune in California.

Merchants' Express Line of Clipper Ships for
SAN FRANCISCO.
Dispatching the greatest number of Vessels, and loading none but those of the first-class.

THE SPLENDID A 1 CLIPPER SHIP
RICHARD S. ELY
LIVINGSTON, Commander,
AT PIER 16 EAST RIVER.

This elegant vessel ranks among the sharpest afloat, and is worthy of the personal attention of every shipper. She stands A 1 clean. Comes to her berth with a large portion of her cargo on board, and will have very quick dispatch.

RANDOLPH M. COOLEY,
88 WALL ST., Tontine Building,
Agents in San Francisco, Messrs. DE WITT, KITTLE & CO.

◁ A promotional card for the clipper ship *Richard S. Ely* sailing to San Francisco and the California goldfields was printed in New York.

LIFE IN THE GOLDFIELDS

Some people who reached the California goldfields in 1848 and early 1849 became rich. Mexican-born Antonio Franco Coronel found abundant gold. In just three days, he dug up more than 8 pounds (3.6 kilograms) of the precious metal. Miner S. Shufelt arrived in the goldfields in 1849 from New York. He found gold in many places. *"It is found along the banks of the streams & in the beds of the same, & in almost every little ravine putting into the streams,"* Shufelt wrote.

Not everyone had such success. By the time most of the '49ers arrived, the easy pickings were gone. Mining gold was hard work. Most miners did **placer mining**. Each miner worked in one small area called a claim. Miners shoveled gravel, dirt, or mud into a metal pan shaped like a pie pan. Then they swirled water around the pan. The water carried the lighter dirt, sand, and gravel over the edge of the pan. The gold was heavier. It remained at the bottom.

A '49er panned for gold along the ▷ American River in California in 1850.

placer mining—mining done in a stream bed, often in a single area

Life was hard for most miners. They spent at least six days a week sifting dozens of pans of dirt each day hoping to find bits of gold. It was backbreaking work. Miners lived crammed together in groups of tents or poorly built cabins. Many spent Sundays in bars and gambling halls.

Some miners described how tough their lives were. Brothers Ethan Allen and Hosea Grosh left Pennsylvania in early 1849. They hoped to find gold in California. They sent letters home telling how hard they worked and how little gold they found. In November 1849 Allen wrote: *"We are still 'dwellers in a tent' and such a tent! Medium horsehair cloth would yield better protection…. In good spirits despite of mud and rain."*

Miners paid high prices for everyday items. A single egg could cost $25 in today's money. Coffee sometimes sold for what today would be more than $100 per pound. And a pair of boots might cost $2,500 or more in today's money. Even miners who found small amounts of gold had to spend most of their earnings on food and clothing.

Miners from other countries had an even more difficult time. They often faced **discrimination**. Many were chased away from their claims with threats of violence. Antonio Franco Coronel had lived in California for many years. Still, other miners forced him to leave a rich claim because he was a foreigner.

CRITICAL THINKING

What are some reasons people might have discriminated against miners from outside of the United States?

There was little formal justice in the mining camps. Most miners lived by informal rules, such as the Miner's Ten Commandments. One said: *"Thou shalt have no other claim than one."* Another stated: *"Thou shalt not steal a pick, or a shovel, or a pan from thy fellow miner...."* Some miners ignored these rules. Theft and even murder were common. As crime increased, some mining camps formed Committees of Vigilance. These groups carried out informal trials when crimes were committed. People found guilty were often **lynched**.

◁ The Miner's Ten Commandments were the only rules many miners lived by in their camps.

discriminate—to treat a person or group unfairly, often because of race or religion

lynch—to be put to death, often by hanging, by mob action and without legal authority

THE VEINS RUN DRY

Most of the easy-to-reach gold was gone by 1851. At that point some miners quit working their own claims. Instead they worked for wages for large mining companies. Some companies dug deep mines. Others blasted jets of water at streambeds. They hoped to uncover gold buried beneath the rocks. Miners **extracted** about $81 million of gold in 1852. Then the figures declined. In all, more than 750,000 pounds (340,194 kg) of gold were mined during the Gold Rush.

A few miners found wealth. Most found only disappointment. Hiram Pierce of Troy, New York, left behind a wife and seven children in search of riches. After two years in California, he sold his shovel for $2. He headed home with nothing to show for all his work.

"I have made an honest effort," Pierce wrote. *"I will no longer sacrifice all that is dear on earth or worth living for, for the hope of gain."*

CRITICAL THINKING

How do you think the families of miners managed during the long time apart?

extract—to remove

Gold Extracted During the Gold Rush

Year	Amount
1849	$10 million
1850	$41 million
1851	$75 million
1852	$81 million
1857	$45 million
1860–1880	$170 million

△ Miners sometimes worked deep underground to find gold.

Charles H. Harvey left his wife in Ohio in 1852 in search of gold. He wrote in his diary about giving up his unsuccessful mining efforts. He ended up working on a farm, chopping wood, and doing other odd jobs just to survive. *"Have been searching for work but found none, Dull times,"* Harvey wrote. *"Do not know what to do … almost out of money."* Like Pierce, he returned home without the riches he had hoped to find.

A few miners made a fortune finding gold. Those are the stories that most people heard about. But most of the wealth from the Gold Rush went to business people who served the needs of miners and settlers.

For instance, most miners longed for home-cooked food and a decent place to sleep. After one miner offered Luzena Wilson $10 for some homemade biscuits, she and her husband decided to build a small hotel in a mining camp. She served meals to hungry miners from a table she built herself.

△ Luzena Wilson

"With my own hands I chopped stakes, drove them into the ground, and set up my table," Wilson later wrote. She used two boards as the tabletop. Wilson named her hotel El Dorado. For her the Gold Rush did bring at least modest wealth.

Levi Strauss began selling dry goods in San Francisco in 1853. Among the items he sold were clothes for miners. Years later he partnered with Jacob Davis to make special pants held together with rivets to make them stronger. Farmers, cowboys, and others flocked to buy these sturdy denim pants. Because they were dyed blue, the pants later earned the nickname "blue jeans." Strauss became famous for his overalls, but he got his start in business during the Gold Rush.

◁ an ad for overalls, showing the tough garments that were popular with miners

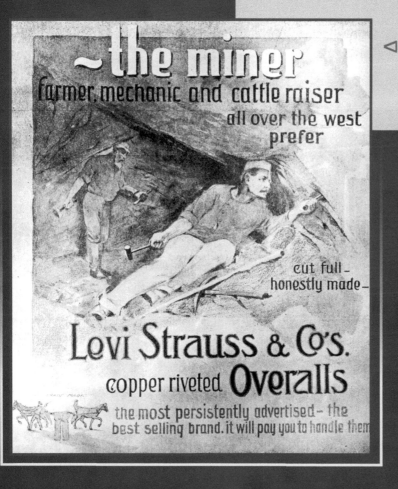

~the miner
farmer, mechanic and cattle raiser
all over the west
prefer

cut full -
honestly made -

Levi Strauss & Co's.
copper riveted Overalls
the most persistently advertised - the best selling brand. it will pay you to handle them

CALIFORNIA KEEPS GROWING

Some '49ers settled in the rapidly growing city of San Francisco. Others moved to towns that were springing up near the goldfields. San Francisco had fewer than 1,000 residents in early 1848. By the end of 1850, it had 30,000.

California became the nation's 31st state on September 9, 1850. *"Our State is a marvel to ourselves, and a miracle to the rest of the world,"* Nathaniel Bennett said. Bennett was one of the first justices to serve on California's Supreme Court.

Even after the Gold Rush wound down in the 1850s, California's growth continued. Some miners returned home after the Gold Rush. But in many other cases, families moved to California to join them. They built new lives as settlers in California.

Population Growth of San Francisco

Year	Population
1846	200
1847	459
1848	850
1849	25,000
1860	56,802
1870	149,473
1900	342,782
1950	775,357
1980	678,974
2000	776,733
2010	805,235
2015	837,442

▽ San Francisco in 1849, the year the California Gold Rush began

Immigrants came pouring in to California from other countries. They hoped to find a better life. Thousands of Chinese immigrants settled in San Francisco. Many opened restaurants or laundries. At first nearly all of the Chinese immigrants were men. Of the nearly 12,000 Chinese living in California in 1852, only seven were women. Over time, Chinese families came as well. The state's population grew rapidly.

Not everyone benefitted from California's growth. The American Indians who had lived there for hundreds of years suffered greatly. First gold seekers and later settlers pushed the American Indians off their lands. Within 20 years of the end of the Gold Rush, about 120,000 American Indians—about three out of four—had died. Most died from starvation and disease.

"And this gold strike brought thousands of people from every place known to man into our traditional territory," said April Moore, a present-day educator and member of the Nisenan Maidu tribe. The Nisenan Maidu tribe lived in the area around Sutter's Mill. *"They overused the area and created drought and created starvation for themselves, and along with them for the **indigenous** peoples."*

immigrant—a person who moves from one country to live permanently in another country
indigenous—native to a place

△ Many miners, such as those on the right, came to California from China.

The treaty with Mexico that had given California to the United States described how American Indians should be treated. *"Special care shall then be taken not to place its Indian occupants under the necessity of seeking new homes,"* the treaty stated. That promise was not fulfilled.

Likewise, the two men most responsible for starting the California Gold Rush failed to profit from it. Neither James Marshall nor John Sutter found much gold after that first day. Both failed in most of their business ventures as well. As they aged, they felt bitter that wealth had passed them by. Sutter wished gold had been discovered a few years later after his mill was more established. Then, he believed, he *"would have been the richest citizen on the Pacific shore. [But] instead of being rich, I am ruined."* He believed that the way the Gold Rush had developed prevented him from making his mill and other ventures successful.

┌─ **CRITICAL THINKING** ─┐

Do you think the timing of the Gold Rush was to blame for Sutter's failures? Why or why not?

△ Originally from Switzerland, John Sutter settled in California before the Gold Rush.

For many people, however, California lived up to its nickname as "The Golden State." Some people took advantage of the state's rich soil. They became successful farmers. Others launched businesses to serve the needs of the state's rapidly growing population. Later the state would become the center of the world's movie industry.

Decades after the Gold Rush ended, people continued to flock to California. They still believed the state offered a chance for fame and fortune—or at least a better life than they had before. As a result, California has become the nation's most populated state.

Even without the Gold Rush, people would have discovered the many benefits California had to offer. Still, the accidental discovery of the "gleam in the river" made a huge difference. It set off a chain of events that changed the state's—and the nation's—history.

△ modern day San Francisco

CRITICAL THINKING

How might the development of California have been different if gold had not been discovered?

SELECTED BIBLIOGRAPHY

Brands, H.W. *The Age of Gold: The California Gold Rush and the New American Dream.* New York: Doubleday, 2002.

"The Gold Rush of 1849." Online by History.com. www.history.com/topics/gold-rush-of-1849

Jackson, Donald Dale. *Gold Dust.* Lincoln, Neb.: University of Nebraska Press, 1982.

Johnson, Susan Lee. *Roaring Camp: The Social World of the California Gold Rush.* New York: W.W. Norton, 2000.

Lapp, Rudolph M. *Blacks in Gold Rush California.* New Haven, Conn.: Yale University Press, 1977.

Levy, JoAnn. *They Saw the Elephant: Women in the California Gold Rush.* Hamden, Conn.: Archon Books, 1990.

Marks, Paula Mitchell. *Precious Dust: The American Gold Rush Era: 1848–1900.* New York: W. Morrow, 1994.

"Paths to Empire: Constitutional Convention and Statehood." Online by the University of California at Berkeley. http://bancroft.berkeley.edu/Exhibits/Looking/pathstoempire.html

Sutter, Gen. John A. "The Discovery of Gold in California." Online by The Virtual Museum of the City of San Francisco. www.sfmuseum.net/hist2/gold.html

"Vigilante Justice, 1851." Online by EyeWitness to History.com. www.eyewitnesstohistory.com/vigilante.htm

GLOSSARY

discriminate (dis-KRI-muh-nayt)—to treat a person or group unfairly, often because of race or religion

El Dorado (EL doh-RAH-doh)—a mythical city of amazing wealth

extract (ek-STRAKT)—to remove

hostile (HOSS-tuhl)—unfriendly or angry

immigrant (IM-uh-gruhnt)—a person who moves from one country to live permanently in another country

indigenous (in-DI-juh-nuhss)—native to a place

lynch (LINCH)—to be put to death, often by hanging, by mob action and without legal authority

migration (mye-GRAY-shuhn)—movement of people from one area to another

mill (MIL)—a building with machines for turning wood, grain, or other materials into products

millrace (MIL-rayss)—a channel that carries water to run a mill

mission (MISH-uhn)—a church or other place where missionaries live and work

placer mining (PLAY-ser MY-ning)—mining done in a stream bed, often in a single area

subsistence (suhb-SIS-tuhns)—a living at a basic level

trespass (TRESS-pass)—to go on another's property without permission

INTERNET SITES

FactHound offers a safe, fun way to find Internet sites related to this book. All of the sites on FactHound have been researched by our staff.

Here's all you do:

Visit *www.facthound.com*

Type in this code: 9781491484869

INDEX